Dissonance

A.H.M.

Published by A.H.M., 2024.

While every precaution has been taken in the preparation of this book, the publisher assumes no responsibility for errors or omissions, or for damages resulting from the use of the information contained herein.

DISSONANCE

First edition. June 20, 2024.

Copyright © 2024 A.H.M..

ISBN: 979-8227274861

Written by A.H.M..

there is a feeling in my chest
that grips my heart worse than loneliness
you've got me strapped, walking on a tight rope
above a cage of angry rhinos
or at least that's how they seem
I hear them snarling, stomping in my sleep
even though you're very hard to read
I still find myself falling deeper
harder in love with you
minutes turn to hours
turn to days
my brain has gone askew
everything's gone blurry
all because of you

A.H.M.

I am counting down the days
to tell him that I love him,
while the attraction is insane
it isn't until after four months
I can be certain
yes, I know that I would gladly save him
by jumping in front of a moving car
but scientifically saying I love him
would be too soon, perhaps,
a bit too far

DISSONANCE

skeletons shook underground
the wind whipped with every sound
my chapped and swollen lips could make
with every rugged thrust of your hips,
tongue kisses and puppy nips,
the ghosts sang out in harmonies
I'd always wanted to stay the night in a cemetery

A.H.M.

I have a sense that
I won't live long
I feel that there's a target on my back
that reads, "should've been gone "
maybe I'm paranoid
playing games with my syndromes
I would rather give all my years
to you
conquer all my fears
with you
to live a life plain
unknown

DISSONANCE

I wanted to fix you
in ways not even I could comprehend
just an idea of a feeling
each heart string I would mend
I couldn't protect you in the start
but I will shield you in the end

A.H.M.

I loved you like a heart attack
painfully
inescapably
fatally

DISSONANCE

in those lonely nights
I ripped the skin from my lips
the tingling of the cool air
reminding me they can still feel
everything you couldn't

A.H.M.

the higher that I get the easier it is
to hear the voices around me
whispers and vibrations of
insecurities and scrutiny

DISSONANCE

I am perpetually flying a kite in my mind
too afraid to come down and experience
this life in real time
I let out the line longer and longer
as my body stretches
growing taller and taller
breaking the atmosphere
never altered my air hunger

A.H.M.

I want a candle that smells
like whiskey and hope
I want to bake a strawberry cake
instead of finding healthy ways to cope

DISSONANCE

I feel so guilty
for existing
why did she die
why wasn't it me
she had everything to live for
before rolling in that day
I had next to nothing
said what I had needed to say
she said see you laters
as I said my goodbyes
now her children are alone and
selfishly, I'm the one crying

A.H.M.

for once I am drunk
not feeling like slurring
I love you's
for once I am drunk
I have the same thoughts
I did while sober
it's scary, y'know?
to confirm it's over

DISSONANCE

you made me feel small for treasuring
every moment with you
as if we would never get another
who would have guessed
the day I held back to please you
would have been our last

A.H.M.

I'm tired of spending my nights
holding back a flood behind closed eyes
pushing back the habits in crimson stained gloves
as if loving you wasn't punishment enough

DISSONANCE

green apple vodka
if I only I could sleep
fireball whisky
michelle
in my dreams
they taste like bad habits
they taste like old friends
maybe once again
we will meet in the end
but for now I will drink
at night when I think
of all of the things I did wrong
in the future maybe
I will reminisce and realize
this was the right path all along
but I can't go back

A.H.M.

that love was always a funny thing
the lasting kind is never what you expect
it's a dime a dozen and survives on pecks
that true, wild love you see
romanticized and marketed all over tv
is quite far from the lasting thing it seems
true love, a wild love, only lasts within our dreams

DISSONANCE

it's nights like these
that I regret not
taking advantage of your loneliness
I know it's too late and that
it sounds absurd
to me you were worth more
than four letter words

A.H.M.

how poetic a scene,
seconds from dying and yet
I feel the most alive
that I have ever been

DISSONANCE

the black apparition moved
in sync with my steady heart beat
fluctuating in size through
my static clouded eyes

A.H.M.

I can't stop until
I smell blood
I can never stop
it'll never be enough

DISSONANCE

I still think of you
those songs and bad ideas we used to spew
I still think of you
those awkward nights lit by cigarettes and sparking fights
you touched me once
I always knew
I'd never forget the day
I'd lose that too

A.H.M.

for the first time in a long time
the act felt like poetry
I pictured your legs laced in nets
cold knuckles against my flesh
worlds away from this place
how different I wish they could be
these things

DISSONANCE

when I'm driving at night
that's when everything hits me
add another line
the streetlights are breathing

A.H.M.

somehow the light
that shines through these windows
is different
from any ray that entered
that hollow room of long ago
every inch of my morning skin
has shed its memories
I've regained the feeling of cold gravel
beneath my toes
a new darkness grows

DISSONANCE

if every living thing must die
must die, and die alone
why can't I stop gripping tight
to sleeveless nights
wishing you were here
within my bones

A.H.M.

I fuck you for the words
you birth into my brain
I tease you for the fact
it pauses my strain
I could eat you alive
if you'd let me
destroy it all in a second
so you could have me
I'm only second best
a night on the road
I'd buckle your seat belt
pretend I felt like home for you
though it would never be the truth

DISSONANCE

I wasn't yours
you had no right
but I can't manage
to put up a fight
I wasn't yours
you had no right
it wasn't even
the end of the night

A.H.M.

memories of you taste like stale chips,
vodka on ice with a sprit of lament,
cold pizza split in morning mist
visions of you dance on silver screens
playing out like atheists clipping angel wings
prove to me without them they're better
you spit in my face
through word vomit chaos
desperate to be right
burning holes into
my favorite sweater

DISSONANCE

I wanted to paint you like a cliché
but you always got in your own way
toppling intricately placed towers like
book stacks in a crowded hallway

A.H.M.

in your eyes I saw nothing
absent of love
absent of pain
absent of suffering
reflecting only light
apathy
I don't see happy

DISSONANCE

you took the best parts of me
used them against me
absorbed all my traits
paraded them as your own
stole my favorite bands and
left me without a home
heartless
cowardess
may you find freedom
in loneliness

A.H.M.

I'm packing up our home
folding unworn baby clothes
reminiscing memories
we never got to make

DISSONANCE

my bones are shattered
rubbing up against each other
I can't even stand and walk
to the bathroom by myself
I have felt this type of agony and
cured it once before
but the doctor says I can't mix painkillers
with anything you adore

A.H.M.

may you never satiate this hunger
left salivating in your slumber
craving a love that will never exist

DISSONANCE

I wish I could love you
the way I loved her
but I can't and
it kills me every time
I look upon your
curious face
it feels like
part of me is missing
and things will
never be the same

There is nothing harder than watching the person you love most destroy themselves slowly. At first glance you think it will pass, but as they days go on, you're left wondering, "surely this isn't where we're at again?" I thought we'd found this cycle's end, yet here it is, self-inflicted disaster screaming, once more, from just around the bend. Like a car crash, it's too late, there's nothing left to do but sit back, watch, and wait for the clearing of the wreckage.

DISSONANCE

I dig my nails into the skin
covering parts of my limbs
that no longer have feeling
it's the only thing that calms me down
keeps this cycle from repeating

A.H.M.

I can't find you in anyone else
so I'll keep searching inside myself
all these years I've kept you buried there
you were always here
in the back of my mind
your prescience envelopes me again
like a cool winter breeze
at 2:30 in the morning
your lashes kiss the insides of my cheeks
I remind myself I'm still worth holding
this time I'm different

DISSONANCE

what a journey
to end up with mobility aids
before reaching middle age
what a journey
to have been loved and divorced
before turning twenty-four
what a chance
for a new beginning
where I can love myself
be given what I deserve
to be made an example
of resilience in this world

A.H.M.

how am I supposed to please you
when I can barely even breath
how do I keep up the stamina when
my heart doesn't remember how to beat
it's unfair to judge me when I work so tirelessly
to treat you, to appease you while suffering

DISSONANCE

I have rediscovered love that makes me forget I need to eat
excitement that stops me from counting sheep
it's through being present in the world
writing books with representation
that I once craved to read

A.H.M.

I know what it's like to live in filth
I feel myself slipping back into it
all it takes is one day to relapse
chronically ill people are supposed to rest
"just sit back and relax"
staying in bed all day reminds me of all
those years I stayed holed up and depressed
that room beckons me I cannot return
time is moving backwards and I can't
remember anything I'm supposed to have learned
from this god forsaken season of life
when will everything be fine, why can't anything
just ever be alright
I feel like I'm drowning again
and not a single person will understand

DISSONANCE

a prisoner in my own skin
there's barely anything left within
my organs are failing me
my appearance betraying me
my voice sounds like misery
where does it all end and I begin

A.H.M.

I long to be inside of you
biblically not metaphorically
I want to feel my arms stretch out beside you
to feel your fingers move in tandem
I want to look out of your eyes
see the skies the way that you do
I want to encapsulate your life
leave mine in the rearview

DISSONANCE

it's going to happen again
I can feel it course through my body
when I reach up or try to stand
it's going to happen again
sizzling in my blood and
veins that won't mend
it's all in my head
it's all in my head
try a bone-saw instead
it's all in my head

this sight is not mine
pressed hands feel not my touch
I look in the mirror
it's you I see
I've possessed you
with my love

DISSONANCE

dead flowers make my insides squirm
similarly to thought of worms
how they wriggle and writhe
through the crust where our dead reside
crematoriums have never felt right
did you know the bones don't burn?
they incinerate our flesh to nothing
while our marrowless structures are left to be churned
to be turned to dirt
I find it hard to believe that even in death
none of this hurts

A.H.M.

does it make you feel like a god
favored and fawned through eyes
you never cared to meet
do you feel like a fraud
pacing the room via muscle memory
forcing laughter through gritted teeth

DISSONANCE

to see your face
is to see god
carved from the finest
brimstone and bronze
mixed media piece
you embody everything
towers will fall
the seas will cease
the leaves will still
when you are gone

A.H.M.

the wind whispered through the streets
as they carried your feet
I screamed over the sound
yet you didn't hear a thing

maybe it was divine intervention

DISSONANCE

to have touched the bones
of so many of those who have
gone before me, what an honor
that our lives would lead us all here
our next destination unknown
the earth, the sky, the water
spread in a place that feels like our own

A.H.M.

when I cry at night
I still hear her voice
echoing through me
so young and unassuming
I can remember her laugh
remember her smile
how I haven't felt them in a while
it always comes back to me here
facing mortality on my birthday
a standoff in my mind at three in the morning
no matter how many obstacles I face
new ones rise to the challenge every day
every single year I am led back here
a new mortal feat that
I am barely equipped to conquer
somehow each year I grow stronger
whether I want to or not
I'm not sure that I can go on much longer
- like this

DISSONANCE

I have staring contests with death every day
each morning our noses draw closer
her hot morning breath tickling my upper lip
it's as though I'm in a red wire blue wire situation
I could blink, lean in, let it end
give into the endless days of tension
or
I could hold out on the off chance
that I might actually swing it
that I might win again

A.H.M.

we had grown quiet for so long
that I began to forget what your voice sounded like
and soon I will forget mine
I fear I won't be using it much when you're gone
you were the only one I kept near
the only one I believed wanted to hear

DISSONANCE

I am drunk
because he is sober
I am poor
because he is rich
and his lover
will be a poor old woman
because he thinks of her
as his bitch

A.H.M.

she likes the dirty dead skin on my heels
she doesn't patronize me for
speaking how she makes me feel
she gives me the courtesy of being real

DISSONANCE

terminal lucidity
the surge
the urge to take life on
the way we once did before
before the debilitation
I go days not able to walk
some days unable to physically talk
sometimes it lasts weeks and then
I'll wake up as if nothing is off
nothing is happening
I never know when mine will come
I feel my surge has already begun
I think I've had a few of them
I think I've tricked my body to live again
every single time I wake up and see somewhat fine
I wonder if it will be my last time

A.H.M.

I spent my life separating
people and things
fragmenting my soul
into malnourished pieces
starving myself of connection
to appease through suffering
I can withstand no longer
everything becomes one
my sense of self I failed to harbor
once endlessly left to wander
outside of me has returned
with new lessons to be learned
to be kinder, to be stern, to be breathless with intent

DISSONANCE

frozen in my ache for you
like a mammoth in a glacier
to escape it is death
to be free is to drown

A.H.M.

I saw heaven in your reflection
heard the angels beckon and cry
for you are not your god's creation
you are one of mine

DISSONANCE

I want to love you, I do
I want to hold you, that's the truth
but I can't physically bring myself
to do it went you can't seem to help
or just don't want to look up from your phone
long enough to help me pick up my shoes
you had nothing
while I had everything to lose
whether or not I sacrificed my body
was something I never got to choose
until it came to saving my sanity or keeping you

A.H.M.

I would like to sink into the earth
and end up in the sky
the ceiling has a heartbeat now
I can't figure out why

DISSONANCE

I felt the moment I began to fall
when you looked away and
my pupils traced your jaw
wondering how it would feel
against my fingertips

A.H.M.

I am not at peace in my body
I wake up screaming and shaking
reaching for someone who isn't there to console me
I'm miles away physically and mentally from
all the friends I just want to see happy
I've been thinking a lot about material objects
and the value they possess
I used to run drills to save what I could in a natural disaster
for fear I'd never have anything of my own again
but my objects are the least of my worries today
I've been feeling a lot like
I would like to give everything a new home
I'd like those surrounding me to have a few
pieces of me when I'm gone
even if they don't think of me when they're in use
I hope I can still feel that I am there in the cup being used
to hold their juice

DISSONANCE

killing the flowers doesn't change anything
the push and pull of tides or the coming of spring
change is inevitable within everything

A.H.M.

I have supported you
I have taken care of me
I fended for us
back in the days of we
the rhythm of sustainability
will find me yet again
whether or not
your warmth meets these hands

DISSONANCE

I wrote you off
I cursed your name
you accepted me the same
I had forgotten your embrace
never once our past
how did we both
grow in this pain
your twisted back
my broken brain

A.H.M.

I hope to piss out all the contents
of all the poison I've ingested
trying to escape you from within
trying to pour you out as I pour them in
you moved on
didn't give me a chance
I was never worth anything more
than an awkward backwards glance

DISSONANCE

I can't change clothes
without the shower running
I can't sleep unless
I already hear snoring
I can't breathe
I can't eat
I can't do this
I'm sorry

A.H.M.

my heart palpitates every time
your eyes fix upon mine
I welcome the abnormal rhythms fondly
knowing that for once
they are brought on by something
I do not wish to control

DISSONANCE

always too hungry for more
you make me want to learn
how to savor you
my heart skips a beat
every time you speak
I'd kill to fill your afternoons

A.H.M.

it was only when you found the strength
to create something for me in the end
I realized you were never driven by your love for me
but by your guilt surrounding others
that's why we never would have survived
in any home we built, constantly fanning fires
unaware we'd started them ourselves

DISSONANCE

I want to turn over rocks
on the riverside with
our jeans pushed to our thighs
freezing on a cool morning in February
we'd watch the critters scurry
out from underneath
free of life's anxious hurry
smiling fully, baring teeth
without worry of who will see

A.H.M.

life is too short to regret loving
to regret every lesson learned
every hour worked
every punishment earned
it all comes in waves and
crashes into us in turns
so why hold our breath through it all
stifling our beautiful words

DISSONANCE

no one loves a martyr
grieving still your beating heart
rid of those it bleeds for relentlessly
regret not your willingness to provide
but all that you begrudgingly give

A.H.M.

streetlights beamed in the mist
through shadowed oak branches
simulating the sun's rays
beating down in the darkness of dawn

how long will you wait?

> how long will you need?
> *will it ever be me?*

a possum gets hit in the oncoming lane
    suddenly driving no longer feels free
    I've lost the need for speed
    the energy to plead
    engine and atmosphere losing steam

DISSONANCE

you were supposed to be here
lying with me in this hospital bed
scaring staff again by sleeping
with the sheets over your head
our lives ran different courses
these nurses have affirming voices
and for once I'm glad
to be here alone instead

A.H.M.

I think we fit together in a specific way
a distant shape of come what may
like slips of slate in seas of clay

I am the multitude of blotted suns
which blinded those before me in
fervor or favor at the sight of
themselves.

A.H.M.

I think deep down
    I will always be small in comparison
    no matter how large my love is
    I will always fall short
    I will always go unnoticed
    I will always be forgotten
    too small to fill in the gaps you leave

I cannot be your soul conduit for catharsis.

A.H.M.

I tried begging you to love me
        in ways you never got to learn
        I tried begging you to listen
        in voices that you had never heard
        I came up empty
        I came up angry
        I came up gasping for any lick of air
        I gave up any sign that you had me
        because my eyes could no longer stare
        at the misconception of who you were

DISSONANCE

lie with me in this coffin of stained panes
hold me as the sun touches me
through colors I can no longer see
as you lower me at last
bury me in poetry
bleeding words
broken glass

A.H.M.

every time I leave you
going home doesn't feel quite right
as much as I hate to admit it
I'd rather sleep on your broken futon
than in my own bed at night
when I wake up by myself
reach to my side in the dark
it feels as though I'm empty
better yet, missing a vital part

DISSONANCE

I would have fastened you a pair of dentures
with teeth ripped straight from jaw
likely without any anesthetic
you always preferred my suffering raw
a steady drip of my self-confidence
connects my heart to yours
at least allow me antiseptic so I can
wash my unsanitary fluids from your nerves

A.H.M.

every time you undress
we regress to jaded loneliness
surrounded by all the things we lost
before we had been found
sadistic secret fantasies
bourbon scented memories
sugar coated shroud of a wedding gown
shed in jersey sheets

DISSONANCE

I let you put your ink in me though
our love languages couldn't be exchanged
you only ever wanted matching brands
I'll always have a piece of you within me
while you pretend that we're still friends

A.H.M.

I'm the *negative voice in the back of your mind*
encouraging you to get out of bed and try
I'm the annoying object who waits in a room
for the end of your shift to complain to you
to ask you how you are and what you ate
if I didn't have time to pack your lunch away
what I could do to help while you're still awake
for the three and half hours I get to spend with you
at the end of your day

DISSONANCE

there's so much blood today
I was afraid there would be
it's light in color, little cause for concern
it still makes me wonder
when is it going to be my turn
to finally get better, no longer live in hurt

A.H.M.

it is all temporary
the good the bad the unhealthy
everything is temporary
even the pain, even the wealthy
do not hang on tightly
to fleeting things
it's best to avoid
transitional stings
but again
it's all temporary
whether bathed in silence or screams
at the end of all things

DISSONANCE

the rhythmic tap of tectonic shifts
cascading over my brain
the faults and cracks the pieces left
of my rattled mind's damaged cage
how easy to open the lopsided gate
free it from its confinement
a lucid image I must reject
in search of new alignment

A.H.M.

this feeling never stops
I wish someone would
pull me off this endless ride
I feel it in my gut
same old mut
fallen into the same old rut
that we've been caught in
over a thousand fucking times

DISSONANCE

stop giving every piece of yourself
to any ear that will listen or hand that will grasp
cease to reach out with no answer
and find new comforts in the past
heal its wounds within you forcing your trembling hands
so that they might rest and still against you
like your feet freshly buried under grains of sand

A.H.M.

I loved you like a dog
you treated me like a stray
as if my broken body
was reason enough
to throw me in the bay

   - *mercy killing*

DISSONANCE

a sadness so violent
it physically manifested
destroying me slowly
from inside of my mind
erratic nights of loneliness
cries too impetuous to be left
unpunished

A.H.M.

my shower beer, my new best friend
wish I could never hear from you again
these silenced screams don't feel the same
when it's now my own hands that keep my head
face down against the drain

DISSONANCE

I hate taking off my shoes at night
when I come home alone
seeing my pair with all of theirs by the door
reminds me of different times, not better times
but of the lives I lived before
I can barely stand my own belongings
disbanded communities for which I'm longing
tell me
is there ever anything more than
this seemingly constant revolving door?

How could a feeling so palpable only exist within me when it is what tethered me to you, does the knot not rest inside your soul? Did you not experience that disemboweling pull?

DISSONANCE

for every borderline black eye
    bloody lip and yellowing bruise
    I wonder how many of those nights were you lying too
    how could you never wake up
    when I've seen your eyes dart open at every dawn's break
    to pull back the curtain and turn a podcast on again
    how could you sleep through
    every elbow
    every fist
    if you woke up to tapping on the window
    rattling of leaves and twigs
    I'll convince myself to still believe
    you wished every time you'd missed
    and nights you'd say you love me
    and turn to sleep without a kiss

A.H.M.

why did you pet me if
you couldn't take me home
you gave me a glimpse into
what the others were running from
I'd never understand why
they'd abandon all your love
unless that one solid second is
what made them stay so long

DISSONANCE

"there is not enough of me to give to you"
even though I said it could be enough
we both knew that it wasn't true
there's not enough of you to give to me
do you know yourself
are you becoming who you want to be
when you get there will you ever think
turn back around to see
if I'm still there, if I'm still waiting
"are you finally ready for a piece?"

I miss living in a city
and having things to do
I miss walking around downtown
but I no longer miss you

DISSONANCE

age does not signify a trophy
we are all moving through time
on our own time simultaneously
what happened to you
what happened to me
somewhat predetermining our accomplishment speeds
the beauty of the human experience
all of us enduring, at the same time,
different things
there is no clock, release your worries
one day at a time, with care, take it easy
we're all still writing our own stories

A.H.M.

after every other procedure
I woke up wondering if someone was waiting
whether or not they had reached out
checked in to see how I was doing
this time I regained consciousness
took great relief in the calm
knowing there was no one there
the assurance that I was all I had all along
it's what drove me to relive
that and the personable nurses
never pleading for any help again
I went to the bathroom by myself
read a book, reviewed some verses
discovered my repaired peripheral scope
in hospital bed laudably medicated and alone

DISSONANCE

stop pouring yourself endlessly
into the cups of those who
leave them to rest for weeks
on their nightstand
empty

A.H.M.

relationships are more about compatibility and trust
than they are about love
it's a hard pill to swallow
it's left me feeling stuck
in the beginning things seem to mesh fine
yet historically overtime I start to realize
things never really did fit quite right
what matters in love
if you don't have the capability to speak
when their tongue only knows how to twist between your
teeth
you will never hear whisperings of the answers you seek
what matters in love
if you're forced to hold back
stifling yourself to make up for
matching what they lack

DISSONANCE

the red captivates me
how it glitters and glistens in the fog
beckoning me to leave this place
to give up to, find a god
the light has taken hold of me
my eyes thicken with a gloss
my expression unwavering
relieved of exhaust

A.H.M.

you once grated the dead skin from
the bottom of my handicapped heels
yet somehow along the way the heaviness of helping
to tend to my wounds became too real

DISSONANCE

when you tell me to stop eating
is it for my sake or for yours
I'm losing track of all the good things
I just can't tell with you anymore
I wish I had never let you see me
what I looked like once before

A.H.M.

something's got to give
whenever getting dinner with friends
starts to feel like utter shit

DISSONANCE

I'm still angry
I'm angry at the privilege of purposeful ignorance
I'm angry that I've been conversationally complicit
that extra five could save someone's life
who lives day to day with on ramp ceilings
grappling with starvation and
if their survival has any meaning.
what are you willing to fight for
outside of yourself is there anything
you would try for
even die for
you fantasize about false grueling strife
while someone loses their life outside tonight
they are beaten, they are robbed
they are murdered without cause
and you sit idly on your phone
thinking "poor me" in your home
no square footage, no descriptions
no price points, go back and listen
just a home, you have a home
you have a fucking home
you have a fucking home

A.H.M.

you wear your mask inside your skin
so you'll surgically fit in with those
surrounding every hole you're in
with no understanding
of where you've been

DISSONANCE

this empty space beside me
seems so much larger than before
you and I could sleep next to each other
without touching
like I longed for with others before
just breathe next to me
listening to our heart beats
heavy eyes and separate sides
come back
sleep next to me
I feel nauseous when I think of sex
yet also if I don't know
when I'll see you next
come back
let's sleep
there's so much room next to me

I would consume the ground
you walk upon
swallow crumbs of gravel
chip my teeth
digest each footstep on your street

DISSONANCE

it never ends
    I never make it out
    no light at the end of the tunnel
    only temporary torches
    they've burnt my fingers too many times
    to bare to reach for another
    it never ends
    this sempiternal slumber

I want to wake up in rooms that don't
exist anymore.

vastness, empty
    that is what you are
    nothing short of a blank canvas
    one eighth of the way
    up to par
    my traumatic ties to you
    nothing short of bizarre

A.H.M.

you are good because
you lack the substance
to be anything but
you could never put in
the effort it takes
to be unkind

DISSONANCE

you are my last coffee stain
you are the blade against my veins
pulling and pooling
without a second thought
leaving an empty pot

A.H.M.

I want to shower
but I may drown
I hope your ears
never escape the sound
of my last breath
that I may breathe
my lips still victim to muscle memory
forming each letter in your name

DISSONANCE

I am reaping every quality in myself
that I've resewn
to sustain a person that will never
hold me long enough
to every really let me go

A.H.M.

I have smoked and I have drank
put myself through all that I cannot take
I never fell but I can't stand without
a friendly helping hand
I have seen you
cough through the pain
I ignored it all the same
I have loved you just as she
I know that you're not good for me
I'm here
not in the clear
running from everything
inside of me
even I can see
it's in my genes

DISSONANCE

the embodiment of Jupiter
a marvel for visual engagement
a ray of sunshine reflecting
blue green hues onto the pavement
a pocket of heat
on a crisp morning
cast over a lawn chair
in early spring

A.H.M.

who are you behind closed doors?
would you treat me like a "back alley whore"?
who are you when no one else is around?
will you try to kick me or pick me up when I'm down?
how do I know you're not just like him?
words only go so far
when I've seen the things I've heard through actions
I want to believe that you are good
you will never be understood

DISSONANCE

you forcibly placed me in a position of power
then adopted an anarchist mentality
put the keys to the kingdom in my lap
then burned down every building

A.H.M.

you used to melt cheese on top of my omelets like no one had
done for me before
          you can't care less whether I eat or not, I still only sit in the
broken chair

DISSONANCE

I heard the church bells outside ringing
pictured the pale choir of angels singing
yet felt next to nothing in return
then thought "my god" this is absurd

A.H.M.

I'd take you any way you'd have me
if you'd let me, if you want me to
I know at times it can be scary, a little offbeat
when you're only used to sleeping here alone
but I just want to be here next to you
to exhaustedly breathe the same air that you do

DISSONANCE

I want everything and nothing
give me your everything and nothing
run on sentences and leagues of silence
stare straight through me with closed eyelids
I want your everything and nothing
give me everything and nothing
either way it's something

A.H.M.

when it rains
may their remains
seep into your every harvest
rotting you from the inside out
in time you shall be the discarded carcass

DISSONANCE

performative comradery
ignorant to atrocities
outside of anything
from which you benefit

A.H.M.

I never thought we'd end up out here back in the rain
always counting on excuses to make up for the pain
I never thought I'd be reduced to a pastime but before you
turned away
you just looked at me
you just looked at me and said
"I never wanted it to end up this way
I can't erase all things I did or
things you pushed me to say
despite your efforts I never felt genuinely loved
despite your efforts you were
never going to be enough for me
does that not sting?"
I retreated back to bed
I laid back down in the grass
staring up at the moon's face
each crater boring back
into holes that are soon replaced
receding, molding, melting into
something callous and blank
I feel the surface fully close and cease
the source of my misreckoning

DISSONANCE

can I sink into the stars
should the ground beneath me begin to shake
would it eventually cave in
everything I worked to build and make fit
if a mouth no longer exists
will the rain still find its way in
is it possible for one to drown inwards
under waves of unspilled tears and spit
flooded with formaldehyde
in a jar on which you'd bid

A.H.M.

I fell asleep outside again
I'll force myself to get groceries in the morning
I fell asleep again outside
I don't know why there's
enough hours in the day
to keep me from circling back
to feeling this way

DISSONANCE

I feel at home here

the mold

so similar to the things I love, the things I have, what I tried to keep
a distance from
    as if we started over on the same page
    not quite square one but something in between
    remembering who we are, the things we loathe, "what makes
me - me"

the tax

this room feels like home, like it could very well be my own in
another life, a different time
    I feel at ease, but now we're sharing dark dreams on the same
sheets, I'm beginning to wonder is it us or this place?

the bags

I feel at home here

A.H.M.

the door creaks and my chest swells
not fully knowing what's coming
you envelope me completely
suddenly I feel like I'm starting to boil
my skin is crawling
I feel like sobbing
it's bittersweet out on the street
to be held by someone once so dear
who will never understand
the weight of everything I bare

DISSONANCE

I admire the way they live loudly
rattling doors and creaking floors
each footstep thudding without hesitation
the sounds scare me
I welcome them anyways
in hopes I as well
may live as loudly
just the same

A.H.M.

you've had a little more
let it be enough
you've had a little more
things may always be this tough
you've had a little more
your voice is turning gruff
you've had a little more
I've stopped trying to catch up
I wish you'd closed the door
I want to see you still grow up
you say it's just a phase
that one day you'll finally stop
you've had a little more
let this be the last drop
you're violently depressed
haven't left this house in days
now that there's nothing left
you'll give up, finally close the door
tomorrow night you'll start again

DISSONANCE

I should be so thankful
to be so full
yet unwhole
I can't escape the image
of my weary fist
flying through the back
of my muddled skull

A.H.M.

I think something is wrong with my body
or maybe it's just finally becoming right
I'm unsure what I'm supposed to feel
when I look somebody in the eye
or when their hand
begins to graze my thigh
I'm unsure if it's because I've been married
I've experienced unconditional physical acceptance
or if I always should have hesitated more
when inviting intimate advancements
every compliment rings
they are deafening
every fingerprint stains
they don't feel temporary
I don't want to shower
I want to be covered by
the hands of every person
willing to commit to the nothing I offer them
I want to be reminded
of everything I endured
to become all of the people
by which I've been burned

DISSONANCE

I long for the presence of someone who makes each day
feel like waking up on an ice-skating rink
no mental delay
straight to gliding
scraping
forming figure eights
breathing easily
in deeply
the crisp cold air
recognizing them from the sidelines
just by the back of their hair
energetically effortless
each turn like a breeze
it's their voice that would call out to me
should I fall onto my knees

A.H.M.

I sat with you in thought of
how sweet it could be
to experience your love seeing my own
willingness to want within your arms
still in cruelty unwavering
you never meant me any harm

DISSONANCE

in some sadistic way
being with you was like self-harming which
I'd often compare to dropping books in a crowded hallway
they hit the ground and suddenly everyone disappears
all that's present in the moment is urgency
urgency and books
no thought of surrounding looks
in a strange way you saved me from myself
your every want, every need
all-consuming of me
every second of every day filled with urgency
urgency to please, urgency to feed
your nativity rotted and you wore its skin well
but you've been gone and the dust has settled
now every day I'm left with a new level
of comfort in my nervous system
my instincts free now to listen
though the sense of impending death lingers
its claws have replaced yours on my neck
the urgency builds again
only this time
for needs that cannot be met
- by me

A.H.M.

I am the two headed calf
expecting twice your love because
I gave it twice the effort
despite all the odds stacked against us
but you couldn't handle the sight of me
the overflow from within as a physical extension
when the morning came
you had your way
you made my exit

DISSONANCE

there's a bitter sweetness in
becoming so close with someone
that you both stop performing
for one another
a sense of loss and
a sense of accomplishment
in knowing
all of who you are
seeing me
for all of who I am

A.H.M.

the guilt rises from within
sending rippling waves beneath my skin
a Russian doll
I peel off the flesh
in the morning a new layer glistens
too many identities to follow
I am legion, I am hollow
I am everything and nothing
all at once, another pill to swallow
falling victim to invalidation
that I hate, I perpetuate
I am unsure which parts of me are real
and which are make believe
who is what stood before
which parts of me did my anxieties conceive

DISSONANCE

some days I miss being alone
not having to be worried about people comparing us
or wanting to tear my hair out while on the phone
no one gives equal compliments anymore
and I swear it's driving me mad
"you're lucky to have him"
"don't fuck this up"
do I really seem that bad?
we can't be lucky enough just to have each other?
I'm fucking fed up of being everyone's therapist
a plausible placeholder made a passable parent
barely ever getting more than an ounce of recognition
for all the shit and turmoil that I've put myself through
god damn I miss being alone
somehow, I swear I'll see this through
because I could never miss being alone
more than I'd miss you
- but I lied *(didn't I?)*

A.H.M.

when the honey had dried in our jar
I knew it was time to set you free
I peeled the wax unbinding the seal,
our time was truly draining

DISSONANCE

I wish you could've met the woman I was
not the man I'd become
she was just your type
lit up every room
outgoing and bright
before everything got fucked

A.H.M.

the sun dances without a care
its light shines through its teeth
and every atom moves on through
buzzing in sensation over the thrilling heat
the sun never sets too full of fascination
to ever tire of what's below
the moon dies waiting patiently
frozen and fearing in the cold

DISSONANCE

I keep a shovel in my car
never letting my guard down
enough to let you in
I'd have to rearrange the way your limbs sit
if that ever happened
trying to ignore the sound clanking
in every conversation

A.H.M.

so codependent
it makes me sick
to love others so much that
it spirals into hatred for myself
through their eyes inside my head

DISSONANCE

do come inside
pick your art
your favorite parts
of me

my nails
my hair
my teeth

could make for a pretty wreath
to hang with all your trophies

A.H.M.

I long to tear into your lower jaw
so that our bones may finally intertwine
too impatient to lie tangled only in your arms
till the decomposition state of life